"THE EXTRAORDINARY WOMAN:
How to become a Be More and Do More Kind of Lady"

BY Muriel Kakoni *aka Miss Purple*

Published by Createspace

ISBN: 9781520772585

Miss Purple Group - Inspiring and empowering women to be more and do more

Sign up for my online course **"FREEDOM PILLARS"** – to help you free yourself from the mind blocks that are holding you and your life back from getting the success you know you are meant for.

www.murielkakoni.co.uk ; www.misspurplegroup.com

Contact details

info@murielkakoni.com

Engage with me and other readers, post your reviews @ www.facebook.com/misspurplewrites

CONTENTS

FOREWORD by Arinola Araba, Founder of BMoneyWize©

It started off on December 13th, 2016, on a Monday morning with an exciting tour of the local Barking and Dagenham library in London Essex with Muriel. I said, "Muriel, I have never had the opportunity to write a foreword before, so let's find out what we need to do!" So, we approached the customer service desk in the library and spoke to one of the librarians, and I said, "Listen, Madam, you are the one who has all the answers to what I need!" she said: "What is it?" I said: "I need you to help me find out how to write a foreword for a book!" She started laughing! "How to write a foreword?!" she said.

"I don't know, well, it's now in your hand! Can I let you handle this; can you solve this problem for us?" I asked. She replied: "Oh, yes by all means!" Muriel and I both started laughing!

Such is the kind of environment; you can expect to be in when you are in company with Muriel! I love the way she speaks her English with a sweet French accent. She has such a fire in her! She is a woman on a mission and nothing will stop her!

I admired her consciousness and I think that's something that anyone would want to emulate. She takes her health very seriously and I love the way she called herself Miss Purple! One of the other things that drawn me to her is how she promotes her skin products and say "Let your skin do the talking!" On many occasions when I met up with her, I would say "Hello, Madam, "Let your skin do the talking!" She was serious about this as far as she was concerned.

I get excited when I am in discussions with her; we come up with these crazy ideas on how to move forward with our goals and I have enjoyed a lot of our business meetings when we brainstormed; writing the book. Yeah, it has been an amazing journey!

I would like to invite you into the world of Muriel Kakoni; just listen to her French accent; it is electric!

This book, Muriel wrote so passionately,
"THE EXTRAORDINARY WOMAN: how to become a "be more and do more kinds lady" is so relevant in the context we are in. Indeed, the pressures and challenges of the modern life call for a different kind of woman. A woman, who is multi-tasking, well equipped to cope with different roles, tasks and responsibilities in addition to fulfilling "traditional feminine duties."

In today's world, we are bombarded with stereotypes of what a woman should look like with pressures from fashion, the media and the marketplace; we are told we can be everything and do more. I think that to some extent women were built differently from men and should play unique roles. If these roles are lost, we are at risk of having a society which is not enriching the future generation. Indeed, it is a well-proven fact that when women take up positions to make an impact; they have the future generations in mind.

Personally, in the early part of my life; I struggled with the usual stereotypes of what a woman should be like. Like most women, I struggled with self-confidence and image issues. Fortunately, I found self-acceptance in going back into the Word of God by relating to God on a personal level.

I am a mum to 3 exciting young adults: aged 17, 19 and 21. I got divorced 13 years ago due to episodes of violence in my marriage, which took toll on my thinking, my body, my image and my self-esteem. It has been a long journey of healing to have come to where I am today. I am thankful to God who has given me a second chance to make something out of myself.

I pray this book will bring hope to you in every sphere of life! And when you pick it up, you find something you can relate to, something that brings encouragement, counsel and direction.

To all you lovely women, for whom life and society are demanding more of!

To women who are broken, tearful and wondering if there's more,

To single parents who are struggling to cope with the competing demands on their time and energy,

To women who are still on the journey to identify their unique calling or role in life!

Thank you, Muriel, all the best!

This is Arinola; signing out!!!

ACKNOWLEDGEMENTS

The completing of this undertaking could not have been possible without the support of Pastor Tunji Olujimi, who has helped me to believe that I could write my first book!

To all relatives, friends, and others who in one way or another shared their support, either morally, financially and physically, thank you.

Above all, to the Great Almighty, the author of knowledge and wisdom, for His countless love.

Thank you.

Muriel Kakoni

INTRODUCTION

Women have incredible potential. As the African proverb so rightly says, *"If you educate a woman, you educate a nation."* Women are the primary caregivers in most societies and commit their whole life to serve others with love and dedication. They often wear various hats, each that requires something different from them and impact how they interact with their world and other people. Each has its sets of expectations and obligations. Each represents a piece of their divided self, expressed in various shapes and forms.

Women are friends, daughters, sisters, homemakers, helpers, wives, mothers, grandmothers, counsellors, role models, leaders, workers, professionals, entrepreneurs, coaches, students, the list are endless! They are many things to many people. With the endless possibilities of the hats they wear, comes a huge potential! Sadly, most of this amazing potential never gets fully realized. Why? Women quite often get stuck in trying to balance these many hats!! In their attempt to fulfil all their roles and giving their best, women often struggle with unhealthy lifestyles and patterns that drive them tirelessly to do more and more at the expense of themselves. Besides, there are massive blocks that keep them stuck, unhappy and unfulfilled despite all that they do.

As a woman, I know you may be busy with your job, career or business around your family commitment. You may be in or out of a relationship. You may be facing a life-changing event; a divorce, a death in the family or even a health crisis. The chances are, you may also want to be more and do more but just don't know how to make it happen.

Well, as a woman myself, I understand how you may feel to be caught up in a routinized life, sensing that deep inside you have an enormous potential that it is yet untapped!

I was born and brought up in Paris, France. Yes, I am a proper French lady with an authentic French accent as Arinola mentioned! Believe me or not I have tried to lose my accent for over 10 years now, but it has refused to go! So, I have finally resolved to stay real to who I am and keep it! After all, most people love the sound of French and compliment me for my sweet accent! Did you know that apparently, the French accent is arguably the "sexiest" in the world! So, I guess it makes sense, I bring that flavour to any other language I speak, right? It's soft; it's sweet; it flows effortlessly and seamlessly. Don't you agree? As Thierry Henry so Frenchie says "It's VAVAVOUM!" or is it *"Joie de vivre"* or *"Je ne sais quoi?"* (Feel free to stop reading for a search and google the meaning of these phrases if you are not sure what they meant!!)

Well, looking back, I can say I had a normal childhood with not much drama. Though I have a big sister; I was raised as a sole child since my sister and I have a fourteen year age gap. When I was just about 8 years, my parents decided to move out of Paris to the countryside to a new family house, so my sister stayed behind and settled by herself. It meant that I grew up very independently with my parents.

Unlike most children from big families, I had the privilege of not needing to fight over things with brothers and sisters! I had everything for myself. That did not mean I was spoilt but I was pretty much content with myself. I

vi

remember growing up as a teenager; I had my own bedroom with an all pink en-suite bathroom, with the pink tiled floor. I used to wear all the trendy clothes, thanks to my sister and brother-in-law who were Managers for a high-street brand shop and used to treat me with outfits all the time! Food was abundant as my dad used to work as a truck delivery driver for Rungis International Market, which is the largest wholesale food market in the world! (No wonder why France has the finest cuisine in the world); so, it meant he had access to prime quality meat and foodstuff at a bargain price, most of time for free, straight from the finest butchers in Paris. My mum used to work as a civil servant at "la Sécurité Sociale" (Social security office); she was managing the whole café area serving the whole personnel. In France, children don't go to school on Wednesdays; it is a day off so on Wednesdays my mum used to take me to work with her. I enjoyed it because she used to treat me with hot chocolate drinks, croissants, sandwiches; throughout the day. I used to eat like a Princess! I remember the member of staff and clients used to be so kind to me. I was like the little star then! I guess that may be somehow I developed such an ability to relate to people from a young age. Always giving a greeting and a smile. In a way, that helped boost my confidence. I used to admire the way my mum relates with people; always dynamic, smiling. Everybody at work used to appreciate her; she was nicknamed "FRANCE" a pet name for "Francianne"! She used to bring back all the leftover pastries (croissants and so on) from work; so, as you could imagine; there were always things to eat at home.

My mum has always been so hardworking; she has such a strong grip. I strongly believe she should have run a construction business because she is so skilled with her hands; she can do all sorts of DIY from bricklaying to tiling, woodwork; plumbing and electric, you name it! She achieved so much work by herself in our family home that event professionals are amazed. Last year or so, she embarked on doing an extension to the house. She took all the measurements, drew all the plans, chose the materials, and got all the planning permissions all by herself! Though she employed a builder to do the works, she was constantly on site assisting, supervising and giving instructions so much so that the builder amazed by seeing her "uncommon" abilities told her "You are not a woman! You are EXTRAORDINARY! I wished I got that ability for DIY from my mum, but I didn't! Not even a tiny bit!

I had everything for myself as I grew up, but the sense of family spirit. My parents did not quite bond in their relationship and it affected the three of us; there was constant tension; misunderstandings and arguments between them. The main underlying issue was my dad's drinking habit. He had the tendency of drinking each time he went out on the weekend at the local pub and he was out there every weekend while my mum and I were home and by the time he got back, he was kind of drunk and that caused tension between him and my mum. It pained me each time I saw my dad stepping out of the house to go to the pub as I knew once he would come back he was going to be drunk.

Despite his drinking problem, my dad has been the best dad ever; he is so funny! I owed him my smile and sense of humour. He always has a joke to crack; he naturally does not take things seriously. Up till today; though he has suffered a stroke and has limited speech ability, he is still the same funny man!

Unfortunately, my parents kept drifting apart until one day my mum decided that enough is enough and moved out, I was only seventeen! What a shock for my dad and I! But somehow, we survived (just to cut a long story short). At the time, I had just got my A-levels and was enrolling in Business School, so I also moved out to live independently in a student flat in Paris La Défense (The Canary Wharf of Paris). Finding myself by myself at such a young age was such a daunting experience and though I was quite mature and responsible, I lacked a clear vision of what my life was meant to be about.

In an attempt to find meaning and purpose, I went from relationships to relationships which as you could imagine leaving me quite frustrated, heartbroken and unfulfilled. I had not yet come to the realization that something inside so strong was missing. Indeed, there was emptiness in my heart that no one and nothing could fill.

But somehow something deep in me wanted to make a difference and move forward, so I stayed determined and ready to give my best shot in everything I did. I studied hard and focused on achieving my personal goals, kept a positive mind and somehow, it eventually paid off. At nineteen, I graduated successfully from Business School, got my driving license at 21 and gained my first professional work experience while a student. Despite the challenges, I went through; this was such a formative experience of my life which certainly helped me become more independent, confident and focused.

But despite my determination and achievements, I still experienced a void; deep inside me that made me feel so unfulfilled. A bit like it, feels like being caught up in a labyrinth; struggling to find the escape!

In my early twenties, I embarked on a quest to find truths; the truth about myself and about life. In the process, I got caught up in an identity crisis; I was left unsure of whom I was, of my true origins and life purpose. The more I searched and questioned myself, the more I got confused and got the impression that life was far too complicated. So, I carried on living weighted down by my many burdens, looking for fulfilment from relationships to relationships. Until one day, in the midst of another broken relationship, a shift happened! I found faith in Jesus Christ and became a Christian! I was in my mid-twenties and the experience were life changing. I was able to receive forgiveness from God for my wrong ways and choices, but was also able not only to forgive myself but others for the wrongs they had caused me. I found peace, love, identity and destiny and I felt released to focus on achieving my real potential and as I did, I was able to move forward in the right direction and experienced what it feels like to be fulfilled for the first time in my life. Today, I am truly me, striving to be the best I can be. I can be more and do more every day and live my life to my full potential and my passion is to help other women like me to embark on their journey of self-discovery!

As you read these lines, I would like to invite you to pause and ponder for a moment and ask yourself the following questions: *Am I focused on surviving or thriving? Am I stuck in my head and struggling to connect to my heart? Am I living my life on purpose, focusing on a specific mission? Am I realizing my full potential or wish I could be more and do more? Am I suffering from the "could have, would have, should have" syndrome?*

I am writing this book to let you know that you too can discover your true essence, become your best and live to achieve your highest potential. I believe that you can enrich your life and realize your dreams and as you read this book, you will discover everything about you that is special and unique and you will be inspired to start living your life beyond measure and strive!!

This book is very practical. It has lifestyle tips and hints, inspirational quotes and stories which you can use daily to feed your mind up. You will find it to be a useful tool to help you realize that you can be more and do more!

Welcome to my world! "Bienvenue" like the French say! My world is Purple, it may not be your favourite colour, but I hope you will enjoy the feel!

My aim as Miss Purple is to give you the best, something of high value that will transform your life. I want you to feel unique, special and free to express your natural "swaga" with simplicity and energy!

Enjoy your reading!

Muriel Kakoni aka Miss Purple

Muriel Kakoni aka Miss Purple, is an Entrepreneur, Coach, Writer and Speaker (www.murielkakoni.co.uk). Her mission is to inspire and empower women to be more and do more and achieve at their highest potential. Don't waste another day; embrace your life to the fullest with passion and energy!

Chapter 1: BE MORE loving

Let love be your driving force

"Everybody needs love."

Love is the essence of life itself. Love is a "verb." Love is "being" and "doing." It is the essential element needed to foster positive, meaningful and long lasting relationships. We are born with this inner desire to love and be loved, love is only natural, it is meant to flow in and out of us. In most areas of our lives, love is often broken or missing. We often desperately attempt to restore love back into our lives, and in the midst of experiencing frustrations we compensate the lack of love in our life with busyness. So often we get occupied with hundreds of things so not to feel that longing for love in our hearts. By now you may have realized that desperate longing for love in your heart speaks louder than the things you do. Hence, despite you are getting busier and busier doing the things you love, you may still feel overwhelmed, depressed and unsatisfied, and the very same things you cherish start having their grip on you, leaving you confused and unfulfilled. To be more, you need to love more. Your life requires an abundance of love, to heal and restore the beauty contained in every moment. Now pause and ponder and ask yourself: *What is driving my life?* Is it other people? Is it what the media says? Is it the latest fashion trends? Consider this: A car with the wrong type of fuel will break down long before it has the chance to take you anywhere. Don't live like a broken car, filled with the wrong type of fuel. Let love be your driving force! As Sophocles, so rightly said: "One word frees us of all the weight and pain of life: that word is Love."

Accept and love yourself

"Facing you, loving you and accepting you as you are, can be painful, challenging, but it is so necessary!" - DauVoire

"A mother who radiates self-love and self-acceptance actually vaccinates her daughter against low self-esteem" - Naomi Wolf

Love is closer than you may think! Just look around you. Love is there, it exists. It takes all shapes and forms, it's in your family, friends and even with strangers, it's in nature, it's doing good deeds, it's loving yourself selflessly but you may not see it or experience it fully because chances are that you may have desperately sought for love in the wrong places and came away disappointed. What does it mean? It means that you have a one-track mind thinking that love means that you ought to get people's approval or having someone to validate and to love you before you can start loving yourself for who you truly are!

Love is a gift that God gives us; you cannot buy or force it! Instead, if you were to simply look inside yourself with God's eyes, you will find self-love and acceptance. Self-acceptance is the ability to love yourself unconditionally, no matter what flaws and traits exist. Learn to love and embrace yourself. Love your body, your features, your voice, your qualities, strengths and love even your weaknesses! The reality is that no one can be truer you than you. Forgive and accept yourself for all your limited beliefs and mistakes, and embrace yourself unconditionally. If you would ever want to live your life to

2

the fullest, then self-accepting and loving yourself is imperative.

Most women have a less-than-loving relationship with their body. In fact, some of the most beautiful women see and experience themselves as ugly. Other women might "only" hate certain parts of themselves, such as their nose, hips or breasts; others, and this is rarer, are completely accepting of themselves – stretch marks, cellulite and all. In my teenagerhood, I developed a complex with certain features of my body, I used not to like my nose and eyes, thinking they were too big; so I always felt uncomfortable giving straight eye contact to people, thinking that they will stare at my nose or see my eyes popping out from my face profile. I liked my body though, as most people used to compliment me on my shapes, saying *"Tu es bien foutue!"* (French) meaning "You are well built". I also used to get comments like "You walk like a model!" In fact, I had quite a bit of a rolling gait back then for some reasons. I don't know why. It was just natural. Was it because I started to wear heels quite early? Not quite sure, why? Though, I remember when I was about 8-10 years old, I used to walk with my feet turning out so I had to wear orthopaedic shoes for a little while to help correct my feet to move towards parallel. Believe me, back then the orthopaedic shoes look nothing fancy like they do today, the soles were huge and the shoes so heavy. When I wore them, people used to label them "the Michael Jackson's shoes," you know them heavy ones he used to wear in the 90's the "LA Gear" sneakers or biker inspired boots, they were his signature shoes then with the metal studs and straps all over. Mine was all black with a double sole. They helped me with a great deal though to get my feet turn more parallel. Over the year, as I became mindful of other people's comments', I unconsciously began to correct my gait. Today, I still have a tiny tendency to catwalk, but it is more like a habit of walking straight and standing tall. Well, as far as I am aware of!!

Looking back, I did not appreciate the comments about my way of walking, indeed they sounded a bit sarcastic to me. It felt as if I was being labelled as a "provocative" girl. Constantly hearing these comments about my physique and silhouette, though mostly positive, made me feel uncomfortable, I felt like I was put on a pedestal. Indeed, most girls would complain about their body features, but I was the one who most envied. Little did they know that I had my own insecurities!

Where did these physical complexes come from?

Well, like most of us, they were triggered by people's comments and fed from my low self-esteem. The complex about my eyes was because of one remark from one of my best mate, who one day made a laugh about my profile, and eyes popping out and that was it, my complex was born and was fed each time she went on making that "funny" remark about my eyes!

What is a physical complex? An inferiority or physical complex is usually a lack of self-worth, a doubt or uncertainty of not measuring up to standards. It is often subconscious. You tend to usually focus on something that is most often imaginary, and begin to entertain a distorted view of yourself. More women than men suffer from these complexes because they face more pressure on the way they look from society as a whole; which cultivate a cult of appearance, but also from their partners, family or friends when they make unhealthy remarks. Will it be helpful if your partner makes that remark to you saying "Well, it is about time you lose some weight, you look more like my grandma than my wife!" Well, some women hear these comments from their partners!

If someone comments about your appearance or physique, just try to ignore that person, think that she or he must have missed the qualities that you have in you, look yourself in the mirror, take away the negative from your mind and declare "I am beautiful inside and out!"

It usually during adolescence that one becomes conscious of their body and the complexes that comes with it. This feeling of rejection over your body is well founded in your mind, and despite the years go by, it tends to come back to the surface. Some of the hurtful comments made by our peers, parents, friends or partners are still unconsciously engraved in our spirits. Today, most teenage girls will have a distorted vision of their body, and in extreme cases suffer from "dysmorphic disorder," which is when they have an acute hatred for their bodies.

Many women are obsessed with the idea of improving themselves. Increasingly, countless of women are having cosmetic surgery and trying to lose weight to cover the sign of ageing. Why are so many of us trying to change the way we are? If we were to do a reality check, we will realize that most of us suffer from "I'm not good enough as I am" syndrome! This drives many of our non-actions and keeps us procrastinating on things that we know we ought to do, but don't do because of negative beliefs based on the misconception that we don't measure up with everyone else. We feel pressured to not only look good, but also to look attractive and "sexy." I don't get it!? Why would you want to look sexy in the first place? Is that what you want? Looking sexy, means that whenever someone sees you, you appeal to their sexual desires because of how you look: provocative!
Whose sexual desires should you attract, your partner's or everyone else's? In my opinion, women should keep their "sexiness" behind closed door." You can look the part without being provocative, can't you? An elegant look is respectful of your body, but a sexy look is dishonouring your body.

Don't get me wrong, there is nothing wrong in wanting to look your best as long as you accept and embrace yourself the way you are without becoming obsessed with your body. Many women think if they don't wear makeup, they aren't beautiful! Are you the type who can't go out in public with no makeup on? Do you sleep with your makeup on so your partner does not get a "shock" seeing your real face!? Or is it your hair, you can't survive without a wig on?! One day, I met a young lady who had an issue with her nose; well, I did not see any issue to be honest but she did and was convinced there was. She claimed her nose, nostrils were slightly unequal, so she wanted to go through another surgery to get it fixed. She had had quite a few surgeries before which only made her problem worse. I tried hard to convince her that her nose looks just fine, but she refused to believe. I found it really hard to be Honest to empathize with her, but I understood that because she had convinced herself so strongly that something was wrong, there was nothing I could do about it!

Pause for a second and do a reality check. Who are you trying to copy or imitate?
Girl, don't try to be a copycat! Copycats sell well, but they are cheap. If "all things be equal," what would you prefer to buy: an original Gucci bag or a copycat?
You are likely to go to the original one if you could afford it, right? Anything original has more value and therefore add more value to the person who owns it. It's true that we can't judge a book by its cover, but unfortunately, most people do. As much as God looks on the inside, man looks on the outside! That's the reality of the world we live in, especially when it comes to women and their image. Society is quick to judge women on the way they look and most people won't care if you pretend to be who you are not. Many women are faking, acting, pretending to be anyone else but themselves. We put on a mask so we can fit in with everyone else. Who is that "everyone else" that you are trying to look like? Who is your role model? Which celebrity do you know all about? Which trends are you trying to conform to? Listen, if you live your life trying to impress and please people, you will end up frustrated, depressed, miserable and unfulfilled because people keep

6

changing their minds and contradict themselves.

I remember when I lost weight a few years back, many of the people that knew how I look like before, would say "Oh, you look so skinny now, I prefer the way you were before!" whereas people who barely known me would say "wow, you look good, what's your secret?" My inner thinking was that "Well, I don't care what you say because I feel just good the way I look now!" Whether thinner or bigger, I totally embrace and accept myself the way I am. Beauty comes from the inside out and any decision to change the way I look is not down to people's opinions but it is down to me. I don't feel the need to be pressured to lose weight just to look better, but I will certainly make it so I can be healthier. Some people may tell you: "Well, you look just good as you are, why would you worry about losing weight? The reality is that only people who are insecure will tell you that. They think if you lose weight, they won't be able to measure up anymore. That's stupid and selfish! For me, losing weight helped to be more authentic. Indeed, I like being active, energetic and live life to the full, and I don't like the idea of letting sicknesses or diseases slowing me down. I like living my life 24/7! I consider that my body is a God's given vessel and I intend to look after it the best I can. Obviously, you can be skinny and unhealthy... but when you are overweight, you are more prone to cardiovascular related diseases such as diabetes, high blood pressure and the like. I hate being sick so I do whatever I can to live a lifestyle as healthy as possible, giving priority not on the quality of the clothes I wear, but on the quality of what I put inside my body and mind: my thoughts, my food and the like, and I do it irrespective of what others think of me.

So how can you overcome your complexes? Allow yourself to be imperfect and stop wanting to please everyone! Focus on your best features, you may not think you have the "ideal" body shape but you may have the most beautiful smile.

A childhood friend of mine had huge body physical complexes, but was happy with her face features, so she focused her confidence in that area and as a result most people used to compliment her on how gorgeous she is. Learn to look yourself in the mirror and see yourself as a whole person and not merely as a "body." Don't just look to check if your nose is still so long or big or your hips or belly still round. Keep in mind that your charm, mostly comes from your self-esteem and not merely your physical beauty. It is equally important to choose your associations. Hang around people who accept you for who you are. However, it is important to also listen to well-intentioned people who aim for your good and not to stay stubborn in your own convictions, especially when deep inside you know you are wrong.

From today, I challenge you to make the decisions that you know you need to take to be more authentic, embrace and accept yourself for who you are. If you were to set any goals to look and feel better, don't do it for other people but for yourself. As you do, start from the inside out: renew your mind, empower yourself to think positive about yourself, declare yourself beautiful. Tell yourself when you look into the mirror "I am fearfully and wonderfully made!" "I am worth far more than rubies" (Bible).

Every morning as I wake up I make my "I am" declarations without fail, I say out loud to myself "I am at my best physical shape" "I am beautiful inside out".
The fact is that you are going to get what you expect out of life; positively or negatively. If you expect to be ill, you will be ill; but if you raise your expectations and declare "I am well," chances are: you will be well. It is a spiritual law in place; even doctors have tapped into that spiritual dimension and understand that one's expectations affect your brain and body.

So today starts declaring what you expect. Do you expect

8

to achieve your goals and dreams? If you really do, start declaring "I am focused on my dreams and goals," when you start making these declarations, you will be amazed how your brain will become more alert and laser-focus on seeing the opportunities to achieve the goals and you visualize in your mind. I remembered a few years ago, as I was trying to lose weight, I used to tell myself while doing my video workout "I want to look like this fitness instructor, she got good shapes!" Somehow, it did work because today I have achieved what I conceived in my mind!

So rather than thinking and talking yourself out of things, making excuses why you can't do and can't be what you ought to, start visualizing what you want and speak it over and over again until it manifests!

As Dr. Seuss puts it, *"Today you are you! That is truer than true! There is no one alive who is you-er than you!"*

Believe that you are uniquely designed, handpicked by God to fulfil a specific purpose and assignment. Your fingerprint is unique, so should your footprints be. *"Do not go where the path may lead; go instead where there is no path and leave a trail."* - Ralph Waldo Emerson.

Self-acceptance is the inner acceptance of who and what you are, just as you are! When you accept yourself unconditionally, you will see all the different aspects of yourself - thoughts, feelings, images, behaviours, appearance and life situation- clearly with a welcoming attitude.

Isn't liberating when you can experience the freedom and joy to arise spontaneously and naturally to see the possibilities and opportunities that life offers without feeling paralyzed or handicapped by fear, rejection of yourself? Freedom and joy come from a place of love and acceptance.

Self-acceptance is intrinsically connected to your level of fulfilment, happiness and peace of mind. Are you experiencing freedom in most circumstances?
A deep connection to life and God?

Do you feel healthier, happier and more at peace?
Do you experience a deep gratitude and reverence for life?

As an act of self-love, you can begin to educate yourself and learn to take care of your physical body as well as keeping your thoughts and feelings positive and loving. Nurturing yourself also teaches you how to nurture life around you.

Believe that you are good enough. Fall in love with yourself. Accept and embrace your imperfections, then watch what shifts!

Make a pledge today: Declare this: *"I am in competition with no one. I run my own race; I have no desire to play the game of being better than anyone, in any way, shape, or form. I just aim to improve, to be better than I was before. That's me and I'm free!"*

Let love flow in you and accept yourself for who you are without desiring to be someone else. Celebrate and reward yourself, repeat positive affirmations daily, do things that make you feel good. When you are confident in the knowledge that you know how to love you more each day, it's incredible how your life gets better. You also feel better. So many of us hide from ourselves and we don't even know who we are. We don't know what we feel and what we want. It is not selfish to love yourself. Indeed, it's imperative to love yourself enough to love other people. But what does it mean practically? Well, for me, loving myself means I get to look after my mind, body and soul. I take my well-being very seriously. I make time to read, meditate, pray and make positive declarations and confessions every day so I feel empowered to be more and do more. I also exercise and eat as healthy as I can. Keeping this routine has helped me to appreciate myself more and become more confident and do more. Learning to get comfortable with who you are is key to self-love. Pay yourself a fascinating compliment, listen to some motivational messages and read books. Also, it's imperative to evaluate what you are feeding yourself with. I am not talking about food here, but about all the media you consume daily; the television shows, movies, music, the social media, including the people you associate with who constantly speak negatively and fail to recognize the potential in you. Resist the need to fit it and stick with unhealthy relationships. Stand up for what you believe in; don't feel the need to apologize for your passions and interests. Self-love is about getting yourself to a loving, beautiful baseline and sharing what you have experienced and learnt with others!

Declare today "I deeply and completely accept myself."

Act in love

"The greatest gift you can give to others is the gift of unconditional love and acceptance"- Brian Tracy.

Begin with loving yourself. You can't give what you don't have. There are many ways you can apply love in your everyday life. The fact is if you do not take care of yourself, it's virtually impossible to feel and share love with people around us.

Realize that you were created with the capacity and the desire to receive and give love. When you are in tune with your loving nature, you can then direct this love to people and places around. When you fully accept and love yourself unconditionally, you will begin to love and accept others for who they are.

Indeed, we are not just mere recipients of love, but channels also. We are to show love in all that we do. Love is an expression that moves from you to another person and it must be seen in the actions. You cannot keep it to yourself; you ought to give it away so others can receive it!

Consider the following love quotes from Mother Theresa:

"It is not how much you do, but how much love you put into the doing that matters." "There is more hunger for love and appreciation in this world than for bread." "The hunger for love is much more difficult to remove than the hunger for bread." "The greatest science in the world; in heaven and on earth; is love."

"We can do no great things; only small things with great love."

Take action TODAY, show love to somebody. That somebody could be someone you have had a hard time to love: a bitter partner, family member or friend, a harsh boss or an enemy. Love is a force, when you act it, it will turn things around and touch people's lives around you. Start a love revolution TODAY! Open your heart

"Love recognizes no barriers. It jumps hurdles, leaps fences, penetrates walls to arrive at its destination full of hope" Maya Angelou.

In the midst of chaos, difficulty and strife, when you come with an open heart, you will see the opportunity to love all things into balance, joy, harmony and peace.

Your life is filled with opportunities to experience love when you realize your potential to love unconditionally, you transform yourself and people around you at the same time.

Give what you want to other people, be the change you want to see in people. If you want more affection, be more affectionate with those around you; if you need a boost to your self-esteem, boost someone else's by telling them when they have done something well; if you want to be able to trust more, be more trustworthy, really be there for people when they need you. Think about what you want and then look around you and see where you can give it to give it to someone else. This has the effect of opening your heart and mind as you take your attention away from you and your problems and focus on others.

Ask yourself questions: how loving do I perceive myself to be right now? Will I want to be more kind, gentle, forgiving, tolerant and loving?

Opening your heart is never easy, especially when there has been a heartbreak that has shut you down and allowed you to build walls to protect your heart. But RIGHT NOW, you can decide to feel again... to love again ... and to let love back in!

Accepting love

"The supreme happiness of life is the conviction that we are loved; loved for yourself-say rather; loved in spite of ourselves.- Victor Hugo

Do you have a hard time believing when someone says "I love you!"? Well, most women do! They may be may be genuine reasons why you might find difficult accepting love. Perhaps you have been hurt in the past and you are

13

afraid that you may be hurt again if you accept someone's love. You may have trouble loving yourself, so you see yourself as unworthy of another person's love. No matter your reason for being afraid to accept love, there are things you can do to help you open yourself up to the magic that come with loving and being loved.

Love is the greatest gift that anyone can give you. It's so expensive and precious. It costs to love. You may be familiar with the most popular verse in the Bible (Message John 3:16) that says "This is how much God loved the world: He gave his Son, his one and only Son. And this is why: so that no one need be destroyed; by believing in him, anyone can have a whole and lasting life". God paid the price to express and demonstrate His love toward humanity; He sacrificed His Son. In return for this free gift, He expects us to love Him and open our hearts to Him. It seems simple and easy to accept a gift especially when you know that the giver had to sacrifice so much; in that instance, one will be expected to be grateful and accept the God's unique gift of salvation but hence reality show that not everyone is ready to accept it!

Why countless of people struggle to accept God's love? Because of fear. FEAR is the main block. When you have not experienced true, genuine love before; you entertain a fear of the unknown. True love is certainly not common. In fact, I am pretty sure that when you were younger; chances are your first ever boyfriend told you "I love you" and you believed it! Right?! But later on you realized that he was faking it!

If you have previously been in relationships that ended badly, or if you were in a relationship with someone who didn't offer you the same love and trust that you offered them, it can be hard to think about accepting love again.

What we are all really seeking is proof that we are lovable. We want to be able to say, "I rock and I am worth it!". We need to get to a place where we can accept ourselves as we are: lovable, even with our flaws and imperfections. Believe that you are capable of finding, nurturing, and expressing the lovableness inside of you. Choose to love yourself and be lovable.

To be lovable means to inspire or deserving love or affection.
Wait a minute! In other words, to be loved; you need to fill someone with the ability to love you?! That's right!! I don't know about you, but that goes contrary to what I thought until now! I never thought I could inspire people to love me through my attitude, behaviours and actions! I realize now that I must be like a magnet to attract more love into my life and make conscious efforts to be the best person God has created me to be.

What characteristics are you displaying that make you lovable? What type of person are you? Is your amiable, sweet, engaging, approachable, captivating? What is the first impression you give when meeting someone for the first time? Do you know that someone makes 11 decisions about you within only seven seconds of meeting you for the first time?!

It means that you need to help people to love you. Chances are if you are always negative, grumpy, irritable, careless, you are not going to attract much love into your life!

So How do you make that shift?
Let love in and don't block it. Simply open your heart, live in the moment and cherish the fact that other people care so deeply about you. Stay connected, believe you are needed, wanted, and included in the affairs and lives of others.

Let down some of your defences and pride and let others know that you enjoy their deep care and support for you. And forget about keeping score; love others even if it is not reciprocated. As one large human family, it keeps going around and we receive it back again anyway. Bear in mind "You reap what you sow."

Isn't amazing how children can receive love so naturally? Consider how they offer compliments without a thought and they accept so genuinely the compliments that they are given. Working with children has made me realized how spontaneous they can be. Indeed, the most heartfelt compliments I ever received were expressed by children. Relearning what was once innate for you, getting in tune with that childlike ability to give and receive love can restore a lot of happiness and trust in your life.

CHAPTER 2: BE MORE real

Know your "why" for a living

"He who has a why can endure." -Frederick Nietzsche.
"The greatest tragedy in life is not death, but a life without a purpose." - Myles Munroe

Mark Twain, American Author of the19th century, so rightly said: "The most two important days in your life are the day you are born and the day you find out why." Knowing your why is an important first step in figuring out how to achieve the goals that excite you and create a life you enjoy living (versus merely surviving!). Indeed, only when you know your why you will find the courage to take the necessary risks and initiatives to move to your next level; stay motivated and keep going when things get tough. Your life purpose, your "sweet spot" sits in the intersection of your talents, skills/expertise, passions and deepest values, so make it your mission to find it! Your purpose is an integral part of you. You can only be fully satisfied and content when you discover and live to fulfil your purpose. For sure God created you with a definite purpose in mind. God created you to be yourself, he made you unique and special so you can leave your own personal footprint on this earth and make a difference around you. As a civil rights leader, Howard Thurmon once wrote *"Don't ask yourself what the world needs; ask yourself what make you come alive, then go do that. Because what the world needs are people who have come alive!"*

Living with purpose means focusing on things that matter most. Certainly, this has been the experience of Oprah Winfred who cultivated her very imaginative mind since childhood. While being raised by her grandmother, she lived in terrible conditions. She barely had friends so she would frequently play with her farm animals, give them names and include them in games. Not knowing that this was her training ground, where she began to develop her craze for acting. Oprah knew how to read and write before the age of three and during church service she would recite poems and verses from the Bible so much so that the church and entire neighbourhood knew she had a gift and nicknamed her "The Little Speaker," and as you know the rest is history! She became a woman with a sting perspective, which millions across the world want to have insight on. Because she knew her why for living, Oprah will forever be remembered as an innovator through the landmarks she made, becoming the first female African-American to host a television show, inspiring millions of people across the world. Today, she is regarded as an icon who paved the way for others to become successful. Like Oprah, when you know your why for doing something you are on your way to success!

Sadly, most people hate their job and spend the best part of their life (8+ hours a day) in a job or profession that they are not passionate about! According to an article in the Daily Telegraph (Sept 2015), half of UK workers want to change their careers. People are discontent at work. Thousand male and female professionals of different age were interviewed by the LSBF (London School of Business and Finance) and 47% (nearly half!) of them were looking for a career change. Why is that? Most of them are hoping for a new career that will bring a salary increase, better work-life balance and job satisfaction. Comparatively, around a quarter said they had made a mistake entering their current profession. This rises to 30% for the 25-34 years old, and 66% for the 18 and 34-year-old! The latter (Millennial generation aged 18-34) feel their entrepreneurial talents are underutilised in the traditional workplace.

Which category do you fall into? The one who is looking for better-paid job and work-life balance or you just simply realised that you are in the wrong job altogether?

The late Myles Munroe once said "the wealthiest places in the world are not gold mines, oil fields, diamond mines or banks. The wealthiest place is the cemetery. There lie companies that were never started, masterpieces that were never painted...in the cemetery, there is buried the greatest treasure of untapped potential. There is a treasure within you that must come out. Don't go to the grave with you treasure still within YOU!" Myles Munroe died tragically just over a couple years ago, but he certainly did not bury his treasures with him. He left behind him a wealth and a legacy of wisdom through his teachings and the books he wrote.

Unhappiness makes us less productive, less healthy, and miserable in general. If you are truly unhappy at work, there's no reason to allow that unhappiness to continue and steal your joy. No job is worth your perpetual unhappiness. However, there is a difference between moments of unhappiness and on-going unhappiness. Ask yourself: Am I truly unhappy at work or just having a bad week? If you are just having a bad week; well, try to make positive changes in your mind first and in your situation by taking meaningful actions to improve your

19

environment. Indeed, you may not be able to control your circumstances fully but you can choose the way you react to things. Learn how to live consciously 24/7; it means to think and behave differently than you have in the past. To develop and sustain happiness, choose your responses to the events that happen in your life instead of being a victim. Make a conscious effort to see the good in every situation. Don't cry over a spilled makeup on the carpet or a cracked phone screen, though it's painful. Don't waste your energy lamenting or worrying about petty things.

I used to be so miserable and unfulfilled in my very first jobs. Decades ago, I graduated with a degree in International Business which I started in France and completed in the UK. When, I was young, my dream job was to travel the world and make lots of money, so I thought if I became an International Businessperson I could live out my dream. To my big disappointment, my first jobs did not come with international travel and heavy pay checks, but instead, with long hours commuting, and just enough money to pay the bills; nothing extra! I guess I was disillusioned to think that once I hit the workplace; my dreams will come through without trying to climb the corporate ladder. The only times I got to travel on the job were when the very blue-chip company who employed me in the UK (which I would not mention the name here) sent me to France on a mission for a whole month, all expenses paid, to organize an office relocation in the UK; really what it was is that I was given the task to transfer a whole business which was going to become my job in the UK. The second time I travelled was in Belgium for a visit to one of our head offices, again all expenses paid. Well, my dream quickly faded away once I was back to reality on the job; working Monday to Friday, 9-5pm; commuting about 2-3 hours each day. I realized early in my career that I was not going to be satisfied in the workplace; as it means I am not in control but the boss is.

While a student in business school; I used to think that one day I was going to own my own business and live life on my terms. Because of that dream, I never got fulfilled in the workplace. The main reason why I was not satisfied that I had not found my true purpose. I remember having that awkward feeling that something deep inside me so strong was missing: a greater potential yet to be tapped into.

So, I started questioning God... and He did answer and reveal what my purpose is and today I am living it and feel so fulfilled!

An aspect of my purpose is to help you find your purpose as you read these lines.

To identify your purpose, ask yourself the following "hotspot" questions:

What am I passionate about?

What kind of people attracts my attention?

What ignites my curiosity?

What triggers my creativity?

What are my interests/hobbies?

What do people compliment me on?

The moment God reveals His reason for you being here, everything changes. It all starts with a simple heart cry: "God show me your ways!" So today, gain a better understanding of who you are, build a well-developed personal identity and become more focused as you work towards your goals and aspirations.

My reason for being here became clear when I became a Christian and put my trust in God. From that time, I have been living a purposeful driven life and been so fulfilled. When you allow God to guide you to become who He has designed you to be and to do what He has prepared for you to do, life becomes worth living until then you are just surviving! I urge you TODAY to come to God and ask him to direct you to discover your life purpose. God has deposited gifts, talents, abilities and great potential within you to help you fulfil your purpose. The chances are, everything you need to accomplish any goal that you will ever set in your life is sitting quietly inside of you.

Be self-aware

"He who knows others is wise; He who knows himself is enlightened." Lao Tzu.

Part of what makes us human is our ability to be aware of our own existence, to both live to reflect on our own lives. It is this capacity for self-awareness that allows us to see our authentic selves and build our identity, rather than letting others dictate who we are and what we do with our lives.

The stress of your daily routine can get in the way of this self-discovery process. We so often become caught up in the busyness of getting through our day, neglecting to take time to cultivate that awareness.

It is important that you take time to know yourself on a very deep level. Being real means living your own life, not the lives of others. Throughout our lives, and particularly our childhood, we pick up messages and labels based on what other people think and say about us and we embrace these into our own belief system so much so that we begin to live our lives to please other people. We become a "people-pleaser", pleasing everyone else but ourselves at the expense of what we believe is true. Eventually, we assume these beliefs are our own, but the more we seek to please people the more rejection we experience. People are people, they are far from being perfect, and living your life to please others who today tells you "I love you" and tomorrow "I don't anymore." will leave you with scars and confusion.

Becoming self-aware works to assess all these beliefs and values and see which ones are really your own and which you have incorporated simply because you saw them reflected in others.

Once you know your values and what matters to you most, you can take bold actions in line with what you, believe is worth living for, what you believe is true and worth your time. You will be fulfilled in what you do and inspire others around you.

Be authentic

"Be a first rate version of yourself, not a second rate version of someone else." - Judy Garland

What is authenticity? It is simply the quality of being real or genuine. By just observing the way someone speaks or carries themselves you will know in an instant whether he or she is being real unless they are very good actors!

Authentic people behave in such a manner that makes them extremely likable and pleasant to be around: they just be the best version of themselves! I am sure you would rather connect with people who are more real than people who pretend around you!

Do you let your role define who you are? We tend to base our idea of who we are in everyday roles such as parents and spouse or even what we do in our jobs or what qualifications we have. We even go to the extent of changing our personalities in different social situations and acting out of character because we think we must fit in. Realize that by acting in this way you are not being you at your deepest level.

How often do we hide our feelings or pretend we are feeling something we are not! If we are upset, we hide it. If we don't like someone, we fake it! We struggle to express our feelings honestly and openly without fear or shame. Showing our true feelings allows others to know who we are and what we stand for.

My name "Muriel" is an English name with the Celtic origin meaning "bright sea". The day I discovered the meaning of my name it was an eye-opener! I suddenly realized that my name reflected in my character. I am sure that you know that the name you bear defines you, right? Well, for me, it is real... I have noticed that whenever I am interacting with someone and in the space of a few seconds my mind goes wandering; that person will be likely to pick it up and ask me "Are you okay?!".

I also tend that tendency to sense when someone is not being themselves, it is like I have an insight into someone state of mind. You can see through a "bright sea", right? Similarly, when you look through a "bright sea", you will see a reflection of yourself! I am convinced that I did not get that name by chance because when my mum chose my name she initially intended to call me "Muriella" but somehow, she got muddled up and called me "Muriel"! I believe nothing happens by chance! So, because I am aware of this, I try to remain authentic to the name I bear and the person I am meant to be. I am meant to be joyful, bubbly and smiling. Feeling down does not agree with me!

The opposite is true, people can pick up if you are trying to be nice and you are not sincere! So, the best thing is to discover who you really are, and work at being the best version of yourself, letting God perfect you!

Being authentic means you won't strive to live up to others' expectation, or bother to please everyone. The reality is that you cannot please everyone, and you shouldn't even try! Just be confident about who you are and what you do. This way you will attract the right people who value you for who you are.

You a unique individual. You have unique gifts, aspirations and access to resources and opportunities that will enrich your life. As such, your path is unique, no one can leave the same footprints. You don't need to compare yourselves to others. Instead, do your best to remain true to your own dreams and aspirations. As much as possible, try not comparing your progress with others. As a matter of fact, what works for others might not necessarily work for you! Of course, you can use other people's stories to get inspired and motivated, or draw from other people's experience, but keep in mind that you cannot just copy and paste what they are about, that will make you a fake! As Israel More Ayivor, an inspirational writer said, *"A single day in my own shoe that is comfortable for me is better than 365 days in someone else's shoes that does not fit me at all."*

There is only one YOU in this world and only you should make the important decisions in your life. Be in the driving seat of your own life. Make all the important life decisions for yourself. If you allow someone else to make all the decisions for you, then the only person who will fail in the end is you.

When you stay authentic to who you really are; you feel happier; more fulfilled and you experience a greater sense of purpose and satisfaction. People around you also feel more attracted to you.

I am quite aware of my ability to inspire people with my natural energy and spontaneity so I usually make conscious efforts to express my "SWAGGA" to create a WOW factor when I meet someone for the first time!! Your

25

"SWAGGA" is your style or personality; it is what set you apart from anybody else. How do you sound when you talk? How do you move? What a lasting impressing you have on people you meet? How do you carry yourself, what is your essence? I did not realize I had a "SWAGGA" until my coach one day sensing that I was feeling a bit nervous as I was getting ready to speak at a training event told me "Come on Muriel, just display your French SWAGGA and you will be fine!". He was right, in fact, each time I talk publicly, I get people telling me how much they love my energy and my accent!

Recently, I was invited to speak at a friend's radio station to promote my book and as he introduced me on air, he said "I have the pleasure to be in the studio with Muriel aka Miss Purple, she has a VAVAVOOMICH French accent...!".... I thought to myself "Really?!". I am sure you remember when Thierry Henry starred in that TV advert "VA va Voom" for Renault Clio back in 2001; and how popular it was...?!

Well, I had no idea what "VA va Voom" really meant until I googled it, and this is what I found "the quality of being interesting, exciting, or sexually appealing!"
Also, meaning "life" or "passion". His romantic interest in the commercial was apparently his then-girlfriend who later became his wife. VA va Voom was then added to the Concise Oxford English Dictionary! Imagine!!

No doubt there is something "VAVAVOOMICH" about you! If you do not know it yet; do everything possible to discover it!

I am sure you may have a burning question right now: why Miss Purple?! Most people ask me the same question: why Purple?!!

So, let me tell you a short story: A couple of years back, I used to wear conservative neutral colours, such as black, navy and grey! I just did not know any better! I guess I was accustomed to follow the accepted dress code for women professionals in a corporate job! A job I hated by the way!

As you know colour psychology affects our lives in so many ways, yet we often don't realize the impact of our colour choices!!

Looking back, I can say I was quite introvert back then; keeping myself to myself, minding my own business, very different to the "swaga" I tend to display today!! No Va va voom!!

But one day..... I was invited to a wedding of a close friend, and I needed to find a dress I could wear quick and easy. So, I went to one of my favourite high street shops, where I usually buy my party dresses with a friend who is really good at window shopping, to help me find the perfect outfit. As I entered the shop, I kept looking around for the dress that will catch my attention, I wanted the "wow factor"!!

My friend who was well meaning to help, grabbed a couple of dresses and sought my approval... I looked at the dresses and nodded "nah!"; she kept on pointing at dresses tirelessly but none caught my attention... until finally.................!!!

boom... finally, finally the magic moment happened: I saw this lovely cute dress. You may wonder how did the dress looked   like?!
It was nothing very fancy, a simple long straight summery fluffy dress, but there was something so unique about that dress... guess what?! It was purple!!!!!

Yep!! Purple!! It was love at first sight! I got it straight with no hesitation, got a pair of purple shoes and a purple bag to go with it, all set for the wedding! I felt so unique wearing that dress, I felt royal, sophisticated; and for some reasons I felt like I had blossomed!

So, that's how my love story with purple started!! It was love at first sight! Then I got in the habit of buying purple clothes and accessories each time I went shopping; people started noticing and buying me purple gifts for my birthdays and other occasions.

The name "Miss Purple" was given to me by a group of Women Entrepreneurs. We were having dinner together; masterminding over business matters and started to give each other nicknames; one was called "Lady Boss", another "the Connector" and I was called "Miss Purple". Since then I have adopted that name which whenever it is called, it makes me feel good!!

So, what is behind the colour purple?

Purple implies wealth, quality, fantasy and creativity. Purple suggests wealth and extravagance, fantasy and the world of dreams. It enhances spiritual pursuits and enlightenment. Physiologically, it heightens people's sense of beauty and their reaction to more creative ideas.

Again, welcome to my Purple world!

Like me, I am sure you viewed the key characteristic of your personality quite insignificant until someone told you how unique it was! No more wishing I did not have a French accent! Instead, I learnt in life to be aware of my uniqueness and use it to make a difference in someone's life. What are the traits of your personality or your physical appearance you wish you did not have? Whatever that is, I am challenging you to reconsider your thoughts about it because that very thing you despise, someone desire!

Women, we usually struggle to be content and appreciate our attributes. Indeed, too often I hear women say they wish they look like some celebrities. Reality is the reason why you appreciate what they have is because they themselves have embraced their uniqueness and added value to them. For a very long time, I was unhappy with the sound of my voice; I felt my pitch was too high. Until one day, a friend told me that my voice and accent sounded so "romantic"!

Because we never hear our true voice when we talk. We go through life thinking that the sound we hear is the sound others here. That's isn't so. You are the only person who hears yourself the way you think everyone else does.

Know your values and worth

It's not hard to make decisions when you know what your values are." - *Roy Disney*
Knowing your values helps you understand what drives you; what you enjoy, what inspires you, and what you would like more of. By building a life and lifestyle around our values we create a life that is more satisfying and meaningful to us.

Your values in life are your own personal compass; guiding you towards what really matters to you. They are your underlying motivation for your major choices in life. When you realize what is truly driving you and your choices; life makes a lot more sense. When your actions and your values are aligned, you are congruent and life starts to flow effortlessly.

Are you a "woman with values"? If someone were to ask you that question, they will probably mean at the back of their mind: "*Does this woman do one night stands? Does she drink or smoke? Does she "take care of herself"? Did she grow up in a nice home?* In other words, the universal definition of "woman with values" is almost entirely based on what a woman consumes, or lets into herself, rather than what she creates.

Consider this poem By Shauna vert *"What does it mean to be a woman with values exact, July 2013"*

"I am a woman with values, not because I am chaste, but because I respect the peoples' bodies and emotions, regardless of the relationship we have.

I am a woman with values, not because I am quiet or docile, but because I speak up when I see injustice.

I am a woman with values, not because I go to church, but because I use the brain God gave me to consider the big questions in life.

I am a woman with values, not because I "know what I stand for," but because I recognize grey areas and I am compassionate.

I am a woman with values, not because I don't drink or smoke, but because I respect peoples' autonomy over their own bodies. Because I act in moderation, and pray for those suffering from addiction.

I am a woman with values, not because I eat well or work out, but because I don't make anyone else responsible for my happiness and I care about my physical, mental, and spiritual well-being.

I am a woman with values, not because I "don't swear," but because I speak honestly and with respect to those around me."

What are YOUR reasons for being a "woman of values"?

What resonates with you and makes you feel good?

What is your worldview or value system?

Ask yourself these very important questions and listen to yourself as you ponder upon what are matter most to you. These are the values you want to live in your everyday life. When you know what is important to you,

you will find you no longer have to fill many versions of yourself but only the best one. Because by following your values, you live with integrity, truth and you become a happier you. Whatever you do, don't let your role in life or people define who you are, make an effort to remain your authentic self.

Now listen to this story:

"A university professor started off in his class by picking out of his back pocket a 20-pound note. And in this lecture hall of about 200 people, he asked, "How many of you like this note?". Naturally, all 200 hands went up. He said, "Interesting!" He then said, "Before I let you have it, let me ask you this question," He took the note and folded it in half twice, and then he said, "How many of you want to note?". Still, 200 hands went up. Now, he said, "Let me try something else." He took the note and he crumpled it. And he said, "How many of you want this note now?" Still, 200 hands went up. Finally, he chucked the note on the floor. He screwed it with his shoe and crumpled it even more, picked it back up, now with dirt, and said, "How many of you want this note?" All 200 hands were still up. He said, "Today, you've learned an important lesson. No matter how much I crumpled that note, how much I scrunched it up. How many times it was trodden on, you still wanted it because it was still worth 20-pounds. In the same way that 20-pound note held its value, so do you. No matter how many times life will tread on you, life will crumple you, life will scrunch you, and life will squeeze you, you will always keep your valuables, that spark within us, all bliss, knowledge, and eternity that exists. That spark will never be taken away!"

The spark in your life will never be taken away if you protect your values and understand your worth.

Remember, no matter the price tag people have attached to you: YOU ARE MORE PRECIOUS THAN RUBIES!!

Chapter 3: BE MORE grateful

Gratitude is powerful

"Those who have the ability to be grateful are the ones who have the ability to achieve greatness."- Steve Maraboli

Are you obsessed with the things you don't have, instead of being thankful for what you DO have? If so, then you need to work on being a more grateful person.
Gratitude is a powerful emotion that pins you to being in tune with God.

What is the one thing you are most grateful for? Your life may be far from being perfect and rosy; you may be going through some tough situations right now. Life may have crippled you and you may feel that certain areas of your life are dormant and you may not be able to change that right now. But one thing that will help you to keep your head up no matter what life throw at you is gratitude. Indeed, you may not be able to control things when they happen to you, but you can control the way you respond to them. Your attitude towards a challenge; will determine your altitude. How grateful are you for what you've got? DO you actually realize what you have and the potential that sits within you or you choose to focus on what you do not have?

Count your blessings

"I cried because I have no shoes... until I saw a man with no feet. Life is full of blessings. Sometimes we're just blind to see them." - Unknown author

We spend far too much time wanting things. Instead of getting frustrated at what you don't have, what don't you take time to realize what you DO have and count your blessings one by one! Entertaining a habit of gratitude will help you move away from frustrations to possibilities. Stop focusing on how stressed you are and remember how blessed you are. When you start being grateful for what you have; however small that may be, some remarkable mindset shifts begin to occur.

The effects of gratitude are phenomenal. By being grateful you can improve your mental health; your emotional wellbeing; and your spirituality. Gratitude can do so much! It can move you from a state of lack to a state of abundance.

Health is another thing we often take for granted. I have learnt to be so grateful for my health, I realize it is a gift from God!
Be grateful for the air in your lungs, the clearness in your head, and the opportunities you have. Sometimes we develop a better sense of gratitude after we have had our first health scare and then realize that everything is all right. But hopefully we won't need to come to this until we are grateful!

There are many people who are not so privileged, and who manage to be grateful anyway. A friend was just recently telling me how shocked she was when she went on a trip back home in Nigeria and saw some street children playing about with no shoes, wearing very poor clothing, yet they had a big smile on their face and laughter. She said to herself "How come these kids seem so happy when they lack the most basic things?!". Indeed, these children may not have everything they wish, but they seem grateful for what they have. They have "Fun, play, laughter...!!".

Be thankful for all the things you can do. This can simply mean being alive, having a family, going to work, having the luxury of spending a night out with friends, or the ability to afford that new jacket you had your eye on. This could mean the chance to travel or to study something that fascinates you. Chances are, there are plenty of things you can do that others couldn't even dream of doing, so make sure to be thankful for all of the opportunities that you are given.
Sure, other people may have been given even more opportunities than you, but that doesn't mean that you should dwell in ungratefulness, bitterness or jealousy.

Have you heard of Nick Vujicic? He is an Australian Christian evangelist and motivational speaker born... that's his story:
Nick was born in Melbourne, Victoria, Australia, in 1982, his parents were migrants from Yugoslavia and devoted Orthodox Christians. The sad thing is that he was born with no legs and arms due to a rare disorder called phocomelia. According to his autobiography, his mother refused to see him or hold him while the nurse held him in front of her, but she and her husband eventually accepted their son's condition and understood it as God's plan for their son.
Nick has two small and deformed feet, one of which he calls his "chicken drumstick" because of its shape. Originally, he was born with the toes of that foot fused but he got operated and his toes were separated so that he could use them as fingers to grab and do other things. Apparently, Nick attempted suicide when he was a child, but recalls that he had an "amazingly normal childhood".
Nick thrived in his teenage and young adult years, despite being bullied. After his mother showed him a newspaper article about a man dealing with a severe disability when

he was seventeen, he started to give talks at his prayer group.

He graduated from Griffith University with a degree in accountancy and financial planning. Today is a world renown speaker and inspire millions of people with his story.

This is so inspiring! Each time I watch Nick speaking, I tell myself "If he can be grateful for his life and make such a huge impact around him, I have no excuse but to do the same!". I don't know about you, but that tells me that everything in life is possible when we don't let our circumstances or limitations affect our potential. Nick found power in his mind and refused to give up on himself!

Keep a grateful mind

"A grateful mind is a great mind which eventually attracts to itself great things." - Plato

If you want to be a grateful person, then you have to learn to see the positive aspect of any situation. Stop all of the whining and complaining and think of the things that do make you happy.

If you want to be grateful, then you should conquer your negative thoughts by thinking three positive thoughts for every one negative thought.

Put things in perspective. You may be upset because you broke a nail, but you have a roof under your head. Remember that there are always people whose problems are much bigger than yours, so focus on being positive and happy about the things you do have.

People who are ungrateful are always blaming the world for their problems and thinking that nothing bad that happens is their fault. If you want to be a grateful person, then you have to stop thinking that the world, your partner, your boss, your friends, or your family are all out

36

to get you, and focus on all of the ways that the world is helping you make your life easier.

Take control of your life. Stop thinking that you are a victim of bad circumstances and focus on all of the things in your life that anyone would agree are actually good circumstances.

Every morning before after I get out of bed, I think about something I am grateful for, and express thanks with deep feelings of gratitude. This set me on the right vibration for the rest of the day. I would then speak my positive affirmation and declaration referring to my journal. I speak them out with power and authority. I make declarations about my finances, relationships, health, business, family and every area of my life. I also pray. I have incorporated these principles of being grateful first thing every day and have seen tremendous benefits in my life.

For ten years, Oprah Winfrey kept a gratitude journal and when she stopped, she says her wealth, responsibility and possessions had grown but her happiness hadn't. Now she notes every time she has a grateful moment, as "you radiate and generate more goodness for yourself".

Now your turn, get a journal and write down all that you are grateful each day, it may be as simple as the clothes you are wearing, your family, your job. Be grateful for the things that are still coming, like new possibilities, opportunities and connections. Whatever you focus on, you will attract more of.

Chapter 4: BE MORE confident

Self-talk positively

"Be careful how you are talking to yourself because you are listening." Lisa M. Hayes

Listen to yourself when talking to people and within yourself. What do you hear?
How is your thought life? What do you choose to think about? What do you choose to put into your mind? Your brain is made up 12 to 14 billion cells and how you choose to use them is so important and will affect your mental wellbeing. It's about minding your mind. To live your life with focus and purpose, you must harness the 10,000-plus thoughts that pass through your mind each day. That's a great challenge, isn't?

Most women suffer from negative critical thoughts about themselves and others, it's so common.

How positive do you sound? What you say to yourself is as important as what you say to others. The battle to achieve your full potential is in your mind. Are you fighting the battle or are you watching it happen on the side-lines? Do you hear, you are criticizing yourself for not being, smarter, prettier and the likes? Are you encouraging yourself on the positive and being the best you can be? Remember this: "As a man thinks, so is he." Whatever you do with your life is a result of your imagination and thinking pattern. If your goal is to lose weight, you should start imagining yourself wearing your ideal dress size and start thinking about healthy food that you can eat and exercises you can do and chances are as you do, you will be motivated to act to achieve your goal. It lies in the principle that whatever you can see, you can have, and whatever you believe or say about yourself becomes true because someone heard it: YOU!

Listen every day to your inner voice, and when that voice says "I can't" say "I can, I will and I will not be denied!" Be your own motivator, do not expect anyone to tell you that "you can't" not even yourself!

Through the power of your imagination, God can make your purpose happen. Remember your actions or inactions are the result of your thoughts and your thoughts control your thinking. Poor thinking breeds failure and stagnation. Good thoughts and positive thinking will increase the conscious value of your life.

The power of self-affirmations

"I am the greatest, I said that even before I knew I was." Muhammad Ali.

Staying inspired each day to achieve your dreams is not always easy, but it is essential for keeping your inner fire lit and moving towards your goals. Each day spend time actively working on your inspiration by reading a book or a quote that inspires you, listening to music or watching a video that uplifts you so you can start your day with a positive state of mind, believing that you can achieve what you want.

Affirmations are statements that you make about yourself of your circumstances. They reinforce your subconscious image of yourself and help build the habit of success and achievement. They are positive declarations you make to shut the negative thoughts you may have about yourself whether consciously or unconsciously.

Are you saying to yourself "Last time I tried this and I failed, so will I fail again?" It is so easy to get into the habit of disbelieving in our abilities because of past experiences. Disbelief is a snare; it can kill your purpose if you don't act!

Today, start speaking positive affirmations to yourself to reinforce your subconscious image of yourself and help build the habit of success and achievement.

There are various forms of self-affirmations that you can use with frequent repetition, which will make a major difference in your life.

You can use statements of worth which usually begin with "I am...". Use your mouth to create your desired outcome. You must declare these statements of the future as if they are facts. Speak in the present or past as you want to convince your mind it has already happened. If you can see it; speak it and you will be halfway there. Declare things like "I achieve all my goals" "I have a wonderful family" "I have the home of my dreams" "I am always positive and charged with energy." Always believe that what you are saying is happening; the more you believe, the stronger the affirmation!

For some time now, I have been speaking declarations about myself,
I have been saying things like "I am beautiful", "I am financial freedom", "I am at my best physical shape", "I am an author", I am this and that... I have been incorporating these declarations as part of my daily morning routine, consistently. It is amazing what spoken words can do! Because I have been hearing myself saying these things over and over again, my mind has started to conceive these declarations and capture them as thoughts so much so that my thinking has started to be captivated by the visuals that these thoughts have created in my mind. These visuals now begin to feed my dreams and inspire my actions and decisions.

Set aside a specific time daily for your meditation, affirmations and visualizations. This will help set a pattern for you to do them daily. Be consistent.

The reality is that your mental well-being affects your physical state. If you don't like yourself or embrace yourself fully, it will affect the way your body function. Most of the health-related issues women face today, including the stress-related illnesses, insomnia, anxiety, excess weight around the abdomen and eating disorders are often deep rooted in your level of self-acceptance. The extent to which you embrace and love yourself will impact on your ability to flourish in your health and well-being. In other words, if you think poorly or negatively about yourself, you are likely to feel poorly in your body and experience some negative symptoms.

Thoughts are just perspectives and by becoming wrapped up in a thought, it prevents us from accessing other insights and our own intuition. You need to separate yourself from your thought and decide yourself what it is true.

You must build a strong, positive self-image. Stop telling yourself you can't do something bigger than what you already doing.

Look the part

"Fake it till you become it."

Act confident and you will become more confident. Dress how you feel better and eventually, you will start to feel it too! It's contagious! Perfect your posture. How you carry yourself, communicate a lot to other people, so make sure you are telling them that you are confident and in charge. Keep your shoulders back, your spine straight and your chin high. Watch your countenance, facial expressions and body language.

People with good posture also feel better about themselves. Walking straight helps you to feel and appear more confident. People who are less confident will sometimes show this in their body language, by adopting a slouched posture.

Walk with purpose instead of dragging your feet, and sit up straight. When you look confident on the outside, people will be attracted to you. Recent research shows that the positioning of your body cues your mind to feel a certain way, and having confident body language has been linked to lower levels of stress.

I will never forget one day, I was walking down the street minding my own business and a gentleman out of the blue, who was passing by, glanced at me and said "You look so confident!" I stopped, said "Thank you, I know!" Then I walk away and wondered "What make him say that?! He does not know me and I have not said anything to him for him to notice my confidence!"; then I realized "Sure, he has seen me walk!" I am very conscious that the way I walk and carry myself speak of my confidence. Often times, when I speak in public; people will come and said "Well done, you appear so confident, I wish I was that confident myself!" My usual response is "You can fake it until you make it! You just need to learn the tricks!" What do I mean by that? When it comes to public speaking; you can train yourself to appear confident and overcome your nerves. Most speakers feel nervous before a talk not matter how experienced or prepared they are. It is human nature; we are kind of fear. Now, what is FEAR? Someone defined it as False Evidence Appearing Real. What causes you to be nervous is all in your mind, and 90% of it is just unreal; you are making thoughts that are far from reality. For example, I used to think that my voice tone and my "French" accent will annoy people when I speak publicly, until one day I delivered a workshop with a group of 40 young people and read the feedback sheets, someone said "I like her French accent!" I had other people commenting that they decided to do business with me because of my accent, it sells well! You need to remove the fear of failure and realize that there are no failures but only outcome. Someone once defined FAIL as First Attempt in Learning! Whatever you do, you always get results; it just may not be the one you expect! If you don't get what you want the first time, evaluate and decide on a new course of actions and try again with an open mind and a positive heart. Of course, it's important to have a winning attitude, but it's equally important to dissociate yourself from the outcomes.

What we can learn from that; is that the very same thing you think is a barrier; people will appreciate it. Since then, I decided to remain authentic to who I was; and not trying to conform, but use what I thought was a weakness to be a strength and advantage.

You need to look for challenges; don't run away from them! Richard Branson once said so rightly "If somebody offers you an amazing opportunity, but you are not sure you can do it, say yes - then learn how to do it later."

When you stretch yourself to achieve your goals, you get to know who you are and what you can achieve. Only then you can discover your true self. Teaching and coaching other people came as a challenge to me; I did not plan or prepare for it; it just came as an opportunity and I am glad I grabbed it! I have embarked on a journey of self-discovery for years now just because I took some bold steps to do new things and stepped out of my comfort

43

zone. As a result, I have discovered that I can be very resourceful when I am stretched and challenged to do new things! Who would have thought that today I will be writing a book? Writing this book has come as a challenge. I DESIRED it years ago, but had not DECIDED or DID anything about it yet until now. How did it happen? Well, a few months ago, I connected with Tunji Olujimi (do like his page on Facebook!) he claimed to be able to help people write a book in 90 days! I got curious and thought to myself "Well, I had told myself that ONE DAY I was going to write a book, but never got down to do it; would that be my OPPORTUNITY? ". I went to his Facebook page and website; looked at a few of his videos, got in touch with him. At the time, to be honest, I had no clear idea of what the book was going to be about, but I knew that somehow what I was going to figure it out with his help; after all he is the expert! The day we arranged for a proper chat, I was actually enjoying a summer holiday in France! He asked me two simple questions: what do you want to write about and what's the title? I said "eh... eh.... well.... I want to talk about healthy living... help women to look and feel better... eh eh... the title is ...." Be more and do more.... maybe eh... eh...". I really was not sure! Two positive outcomes came out of the call: I had committed to getting on a 7day book writing challenge with him to get my first book published and I was not going to allow anyone including myself to tell me that I can't do it. So, while on holiday; I started on the book writing challenge and the rest is history. You can read the outcome of that challenge as I am speaking to you.

I had to battle with so many excuses to DECIDE to DECIDE, DO and RESOLVE not to quit! Excuses such as "Well, I am on holiday; now is not the time to get busy writing a book!"; "I don't know what to write about; after all, can I write proper? Can I become an author? Me?!" One thing I knew is that if I was going to focus and commit to the challenge, I would succeed!

Smile

"Let your smile do the talking" -Miss Purple

Consider this: "A smile costs nothing but gives you much. It enriches those who receive without making poorer those who give. It takes only a moment, but the memory of it lasts forever. None is so rich or mighty that he can get along without it, and none is so poor that he or she is not making rich by it." "A smile creates happiness in the home, fosters goodwill in business and it's courtesy of friendship"- Brian Lacher *(extract from "The Greatest Personal Success tips in the World," 2007)*

Don't be too tired to smile; cheer up somebody with your smile. Even the smallest smile can disarm the toughest weapon.

Did you know that it takes only 12 muscles to smile, but 113 muscles to frown? That means that it's easier to smile than to frown. Wow! Additionally, know that your smile has a voice. Indeed, when you smile at another person, a warm, genuine smile, you're telling the person that he or she is pleasant, safe and secure in your estimation. A single smile is so powerful that it can touch a person's heart and boost their self- esteem in a moment, jolting them from negativity in a positive attitude. Many long-term relationships have begun with a single shared across a room. Have you ever heard people say that "When our eyes met, we both knew that we were meant for each other?" Happiness is contagious. Always make an effort to smile. You look so much better when you do. I am conscious that God gave me the gift of a smile, so I tend to smile at people quite often to engage a conversation; break the ice when talking to a stranger or simply to be nice. A few weeks ago, as I was witnessing about my faith on the streets with a group of like-minded Christians, I started to engage a conversation with a gentleman about his faith; naturally you would imagine that the first thing I did was to smile at him with a good eye contact; and I kept smiling throughout our conversation. In the end, he said, "I may not agree with what you said, but I will remember the smile!" Wow, I was shocked! Your smile can express what words can tell!

Make eye contact

"Looking into someone's eyes, changes the entire conversation." - Kush and wisdom

Don't be afraid to meet the gaze of someone else; it shows not only that you are a person worthy of communicating with, but tells people around you that you respect them, acknowledge their presence and are interested in them and what they say. Our eyes are uniquely human. They are the windows of our soul and showcase of our attention and feelings. When I was a teenager, I used to shy away from making eye contact with people. The reason was that I was shy and unsecured. Looking back, I realized that my insecurity was only based on what other people perceived and was totally unhealthy to my self-esteem. Over the years I learned to overcome my insecurities and as a result, I gained more confidence in giving eye contact. I came to realize that eye contact is one of the most genuine, universal forms of communication and one of the best attributes of human expressions. An eye contact is direct and expressive; it shows a million different emotions in just one look. Even one glance can tell you a lot about a person's character, especially if a smile or smirk is thrown in.

To put the most effort into showing interest, look the person in the eye and smile. Eye contact can say so much, yet leaving so much for assumptions and interpreting body language. By making eye contact, you will improve the quality of your interactions and appear more confident. You will be more likeable and trustworthy and people you interact with will feel more appreciated. If you can't do it for you, do it for them!

CHAPTER 5: DO MORE things for yourself

Invest in yourself

"The best asset is your own self. You can become to an enormous degree the person you want to be."
- Warren Buffet-

Warren Buffet, the most successful investor in history, has offered plenty of great money and investment advice, but perhaps this is by far his greatest. Don't you agree? Indeed, the best lifetime investment you can make is in "yourself!" In fact, anything you do that improves your own talents, skills and abilities; nobody can tax it or take it away from you. When you maximize what you have, you potentially have a tremendous asset that can return tenfold: YOU!

"Invest in yourself" means that you need to spend time improving your skills, your knowledge and what you are naturally good at, in other words, your talents. Become a lifelong learner and you will be ready for every good opportunity that comes your way. Whatever you do, don't remain P.O.O.R, which I define as

Passing

Over

Opportunities

Repeatedly

Indeed, it is better to be prepared for an opportunity than not to have an opportunity or prepared. Will you sit an exam without preparation? Well, life is a series of exams, so get prepared!

Want to be happier? Then begin by doing more things for yourself! The happiest people go out of their way to treat themselves right and they do something nice for themselves every day, however, big or small. Treat yourself everyday with loving kindness, patience, appreciation and respect, make it a goal to learn something new every day, anything that will contribute to make you a better person and be better at what you do. The chances are if you add value to yourself, you will add value to other people! Remember, you can't give what you don't have!

Prioritise your health and wellbeing

"Your health is your wealth, will you let someone steal it?" - Miss Purple

Most women believe they must sacrifice themselves to be a good mother, sister, wife or co-worker. Unfortunately, they may be left disillusioned and not be able to fully meet their expectations. Indeed, as they overstretch themselves, their unhealthy and unbalanced lifestyle often leads to depression, fatigue, illness and unfulfillment.

Consider this, if you are too busy or too stress to even nourish your body properly, it will affect how you look and feel about yourself. When you fail to feed your body and brain with healthy food, while keeping super active and experiencing stress, you are actually pushing your body to exhaustion. Understand that food is fuel for your body, would you deprive your car on the fuel it needs to take you places? Certainly not! Your car is just a piece of metal, it is very useful, but not as valuable as your body and health, even the fanciest car is nothing compared to what your body is worth. The possibility is if your car breaks down, you can fix it without too much problem, but if your body breaks down, that's a different story. Consider how difficult it is for someone who needs an organ transplant to find a compatible donor, but you will agree that it is quite simple to find a spare part for your car, isn't?

Your health is your wealth, cherish it, and invest in it! Neuroscience tells us that letting your blood sugar sink sends stress signals to your brain. So, avoid unnecessary stress and get in the habit of eating small meals throughout your day, feed your body with good nutrients, healthy food and snacks so you can feel better, look better and do more!

About three years ago, I was overweight and I had lost confidence in the way I looked. Summer 2013, I went on a holiday at my mum's place in France. My mum is a superhuman and decided to build a terrace in her garden all by herself. I felt compelled to help her out and saw it as an opportunity to get active and burn some calories, at that time, I was overweight and desired to lose weight. I immediately called one of my best childhood friends to buddy up with me as she had also been eager to be active. She was up for it and got actually got quite excited. So, we dressed up and got our hands dirty helping my mum out. It was fun at first, but very rapidly as a result of our poor fitness level and the extreme hot weather condition, my friend and I realized that the work was proving to be much harder than we thought. We were getting out of breath, sweaty, feeling achy and tired. Meanwhile, my mum, believe me, was going on fine.

Seeing my mum being so fit, was a wake-up call for my friend and I that day. So much that we buddied up on a challenge to lose weight and within three months of focusing on a nutrition and fitness program, I lost three stones of my weight. As a result, my rapport with food changed completely, I adopted healthier eating and lifestyle habits that allowed me not only to reach and maintain my ideal weight, but also to feel, look better, become more confident and do more!

You too, take better care of yourself. Become more conscious about your health. Make time to focus on yourself, embark lifestyle changes. Your mind, body and soul make up who you are. These are the only vehicles that carry you so you can be more and do more during your lifetime. What you must do is to commit to feeding yourself not only with healthy food for your body, but also with positivity for your mind, and connecting your spirit and soul to God! The new healthy habits you develop will maximize your productivity.

Physical discipline

"Train like an athlete, eat like a nutritionist, sleep like a baby, win like a champion" - anonymous

"Don't think about the start of the race, think about the ending." - Usain Bolt

"Self-discipline is the key which unlocks the doors to our success. Without self-discipline, a person is like a dry leaf carried in any direction the wind may blow."- Brian Larcher (Extract "The Greatest Personal Success tips in the world, 2007). Don't be a victim of your circumstances; but learn how to focus on developing constructive, healthy habits and continuous pursuit of improvement until you win. Success is the personal ability to understand the race you must run! When you excel at being you, success is bound to happen.

There is no doubt that gaining mastery over the body is an important part of every woman's life. And, I must

51

admit, it's grown into a vital one for me.

Why? First of all, because my body is really, truly not mine, but it is the Temple of God (quoting Corinthians 6:19, The Bible), I just happen to be managing it! I have to say that that simple Scripture provoked a complete turnaround in my life, about 14 years ago. Then I was looking for purpose and love in the wrong places and like most people, I did not know that God was the best person to show me how to treat my body. Why? Because He made it! Back then, I did not have much respect for what God gave me to glorify Him with, as a matter of fact, I did not know what I did not know! But, thank God that one day it all clicked. As I become a Christian and surrendered my heart and life to God, I got like a sudden revelation that I was to guard my body, mind and spirit like gold and keep myself from destructive behaviours like sexual immorality, overeating and the like. I became morally conscious of the fact that my body was given to me as a legacy to treasure!

If you were to find a treasure, would you neglect it? Surely not! Finding a treasure is a lifetime opportunity so is your body! It is your legacy from God for you to glorify Him from the inside out. Anything that you put in your body, whether food or sex, it is going to bear fruit: either good or bad.

So, Ladies, let's do it the right way! I can't recall the numbers of times I regretted things I allowed in my body wishing I had known better. But God's grace is amazing. He has given me another chance to become a wiser steward of my body, mind and soul. With this in mind, I place a high value on my body and view it as the only vessel that God has given me here on Earth to please Him with!

Starting from today, develops a love relationship with your body, don't be obsessed with it, but cherish it like a treasure and it will serve you well!

Would you buy a luxury car, like an Aston Martin (the James Bond car) and fail to maintain, polish and pair with it? Far from it! You will invest every penny to look after it!!! Why? Because it is valuable. How much more valuable is your body?

If you want to be more discipline in what you do, start to discipline your body.

Ask yourself: if I were to put a price tag on my body... what will it be?

Guess, what mine is? Priceless and so is yours!

Stop procrastinating

"Today, stop making excuses for why you can't get it done and start focusing on all the reasons why you must make it happen." - Anonymous

I come across countless people who say they want to lose weight, they want to learn to speak a foreign language, do one thing or another... but years passed.... No weight loss, no foreign language yet, not even a tiny effort or action to make it happen.

I suspect you might also have things in your life that you have been telling yourself and other people, perhaps for years, that you want to do but have not done yet? Am I wrong? The reasons you might have given yourself for not taking actions most likely centre around excuses like "I don't have time" or "I don't have any discipline" and so on.

If you keep saying you want to do something and yet you keep not doing it that means you don't want to do it, or perhaps not enough to make the effort required to make it happen. Only your actions reveal your intentions so don't just talk the talk but walk it! It's quite important to be honest with yourself about your actual level of aspiration around doing things, or you won't be clear about what you need to succeed. As a matter of fact, did you know that you can make yourself want to do things?! Have you experienced this before? Have you ever experienced a sudden shift from not wanting to do something to wanting to do it?

For many years, I did not want to go to the gym to exercise, I got bored each time I went and I convinced myself that I preferred working out from home. As time went, and as I educated myself about the benefits of incorporating strength training, I realized that going to the gym was going to help me towards my fitness goals. I was able to make myself wanted to go to the gym, simply by changing my mind about it and seeing the benefits rather than the inconveniences. Now I am looking forward each time I go!

The reality is "You can't change your life if you don't change your thinking," that's a fact!

Dream big, set big goals

"A goal is a dream with a deadline." Napoleon Hill
"A goal with a plan is just a wish." Antoine de St Exupery.

Dreams are pictures, visions and things you think about and you wish to do one day.
Goals are things you take action towards achieving. You make plans to execute a goal.

Setting goals help you to acknowledge and commit to achieve what can seem like a daunting, almost impossible task. Someone once said: "The best way to eat an elephant is one bite at a time!"

You can define your own success. Become a goal setter and be accountable to your goals and make your dreams happen. Chase your dreams and create the life you want, regardless of your circumstances. Often, your dreams may seem so far away or too big that you feel they are not worth pursuing; especially when the obstacles or limitations around you seem like a mountain! Don't think that because you don't have the resources and the perfect environment; it is not worth trying. It is about time you stop making excuses and find yourself reasons why you can't realize your dreams. How big do you dare to dream? The possibility is that the dream you don't dare to tell is your most powerful dream.

Ask yourself: what is it that I truly, deeply want out of life?

Do you want to get out of bed every morning feeling intensely passionate about your day ahead?

Do you wish you make a positive impact to people around you or to the wider world?
Do you want a balanced lifestyle, having time to spend with your family and take care of your physical and mental health? Believe that you are capable of change.

Countless of women wish they could do more with their life, but feel stuck in their reality. Just imagine if you were to say out loud what really matters to you then you will find the courage to do it! Stop comparing yourself to other women. Be uniquely you; acknowledge your dreams, your passions and set some goals to live a bigger life.
It's time you start taking small, consistent, and determined steps to make things happen.
Stop rumbling with your emotions and thoughts and step up. Which belief you have about yourself and your abilities that are blocking you right now? Identify your blind spots.

Goals allow you to get a sense of clarity of your journey ahead, be it to be healthier, to start your own business, take your career to the next level or simply become more comfortable in your own skin.

Setting and achieving realistic goals relating to different aspects of your health and well-being is the key. It can help you become clear about what you really want, it helps provide focus. Committing to a goal actually helps to release the energy, enthusiasm, resources and clarity necessary to make that goal come true. The key is to ensure that your goal is in agreement with your values. Values represent what is important to you; the things that inspire and motivate you. They define the code of honour, ethics and foundations upon which you build a healthy and fulfilling life. My values are deeply rooted in the Christian faith, beliefs and principles. I hold onto three essential values:

Love - for God and others
Identity - Understand who I am and stay authentic to who God has called me to be
Destiny - Discover and fulfil my purpose here on Earth till Heaven, and be ready when Jesus comes back!

I also value holistic health (body, mind, soul) on the basis that my body is the Temple of God and God wants me to prospect in my whole being so I can be more and do more for His glory!

These are the example of values that you can use to set up medium and long-term goals.

To be healthy in body, mind and spirit
To be more accepting of myself and others
To live life authentically and with integrity
To be confident and purpose driven
To do more for other people

You can also start each day by identifying a couple of "today goals," simply ask yourself how can I be healthy, in body, mind and spirit today?
How can I share honestly, when speaking with people today?
How can I be more accepting of myself and others today?
How can I live my life authentically and with integrity

today?

Now pause for a moment and think about a couple of specific goals that you would like to achieve based on each of these values.

As you set your goals, set them SMART!!
Specific
Measurable
Achievable
Realistic
Time bound

At the beginning of each day, think of at least one thing you are grateful for right now in your life, small or big, it just needs to be something that is meaningful to you. Allow that gratitude to build up within you.

CHAPTER 6: DO MORE for others

Connect to thrive

"Without the sense of fellowship with men of like mind, life would have seemed to me empty." - Albert Einstein

Social connection, improves health, well-being and longevity. Fulfilling your basic human desire for connection and experiencing intimacy through partners, friendship women's groups, social or sports groups, your community, animals and nature are essential. One telling study showed that lack of social connection is a greater detriment to health than obesity, smoking and high blood pressure. On the flip slide, strong social connection leads to a 50% increased chance the longevity. Social connection strengthens our immune system; helps recover from disease faster, and may even lengthen our lives. People who feel more connected to others have lower rates of anxiety and depression. It also promotes higher self-esteem.

I love to connect with people; it has become a second nature. I was born to connect. We are all born with the ability and motivation to form close relationships. Children who form close emotional relationship attachment to their parents are less likely to wander off. For some reasons, the sense of belonging means more to women than to men. It is due to our intrinsic caring nature; we always want to care for someone; our children, partners, families, friends, and the most vulnerable people around us.

Where do you belong as a woman? Who do you connect with besides your family?
I am talking about the meaningful connections that give you that "feel good factor"! As a woman, your sense of worth tends to be inextricably bound up in your web of close relationships; whereas a man's sense of worth tends to be closely related to his achievements.

So how can you develop these meaningful connections? Join a group; they are countless groups that bring women together in your local community, meet-ups; networking events; various interest groups. If you have children, you may not be able to attend these groups consistently, but you could look for those who are children friendly; like mums' groups. Meet other women in your community for friendship. Explore joining groups where you share the same goals and interests; mingle! A good place to start to find these meetings is the Meetup App, Eventbrite or simply by popping in your local library or community centre and ask!

Spiritual connection

"There is a spiritual connection to good health; it's not just physical"-Nancy Evans

Apparently, people who have faith or belong to religious or spiritual group enjoy better health and greater support than those who don't. Studies have revealed that attending church on a weekly basis can be beneficial to your health. Though, the main benefits, refer to spiritual and psychological health, physical and mental benefits can be experienced as well.

It is such a privilege to have a second family that you can share your life problems and fun times with, who support you through the best and worst of times. The Church family has developed such a crucial role in my personal development and spiritual maturity; especially when I first arrived in London. I will never forget the first church I stepped in when I became a Christian which was somewhere in Bethnal Green, London, it was so welcoming! The few people I met then, would not stop contacting me every day with greetings, encouragement and positive messages; but because I was not used to be shown so much attention; at first I got a bit annoyed but later I realized they had only a genuine intention to make me feel part of their community.

I met this young lady recently; she is a Christian and goes to church regularly. We had a chat and she told me she had come from Bulgaria a couple of years ago; curiosity, I asked her if she had come with her family; I reacted quite surprised as she replied "No, I came by myself, but the Church is my family!" I was so touched when she said that. Isn't good to know that wherever you find yourself in the world, you have a second family right there: The Church?

Going to church, not only promote accountability, routine and contribute to a more disciplined attitude towards life, better life choices; inspires; morals and good manners, but also promote the services, charity and mentoring; reduces stress; clears your thoughts, after going to church you tend to feel lighter, more confident and free from worldly worries.

It is not just about going to church, but it is first and foremost about having a personal connection with God. When you experience a fellowship with God as the centre of your life you are guaranteed 100% fulfilment and satisfaction whatever you may be going through. God gives purpose, and meditation and prayer are very effective tools for developing a deeper connection with God.

Aspire to inspire

"If your actions inspire others to dream more, learn more, do more and become more, you are a leader!" - *John Quincy Adams*

I am sure you can remember individuals that inspired or improved you in some way. The chances are, these individuals inspired you to push yourself and achieve something memorable and significant or just to becoming a better person. Someone inspired me to write this book. I am so thankful to that person, Pastor Tunji Olujimi who believed I could do it and supported me to take action. Every morning for the last three years I have been listening to Les Brown, a renowned motivational speaker and as a result, I have been inspired every day to live my life to my full potential and believe that my dream is possible! Les Brown uses the art of storytelling to inspire others to achieve their dreams, each time I listen to him sharing his story I get inspired. I realized that to inspire others, I needed to be inspired myself.

Again, you can't give what you don't have! My mission today is to inspire other women like me to be more and do more. With this in mind, every day I make it a point to inspire someone with a word, a story, an action, an encouragement or by simply being a listening ear.

Now think about what and who inspires you, look at their qualities. Find out what make them inspirational and work to develop these qualities in yourself.

I will never forget that episode of my life when I was learning to read and write back in primary school. I can still remember that day where I was given a writing task to complete, but did very poorly in my spelling. I kept having poor results until one day my teacher back then spent some time with me to reinforce some spelling and grammar rules and as a result, I began to gain confidence and improved. That paid off as of the end of the school term not only had I met all my targets, but also developed an interest in literacy ever since.

Get inspired yourself so you can begin to inspire others. Look for people, ideas, environments and knowledge that you find inspiring and motivating. People don't always listen to what you say, but they often remember what you do! Your actions speak louder than your words.

Support and motivate others to keep moving forward and be the best they can be. Know that if others can do it, then it means that you too can do it. Be therefore, happy when others succeed-not jealous. View other people's success as proof that you too can succeed. Don't try to bring anybody down or lessen their chances of success in any way.

Be a philanthropist, genuinely help others

"You should look not only to your own interests, but also to the interests of others" - Book of Philippians 1:4 - The Bible

Becoming a philanthropist, a woman who donates her time, money or reputation to charitable causes can be very rewarding. Many years ago, I found passion to work with children and young people; I actually answered a call from God to do so. I genuinely started to get involved in my local church and community and reached out to children and young people through grassroots projects and initiatives. I have found so much fulfilment in giving my time, energy and resources supporting charitable causes around me, so much so that this has been my driving force and became a catalyst to accomplish many other things.

Consider Mother Theresa, she was a humanitarian and a devoted philanthropist. She lived a life committed to helping others. She served the poorest of the poor and live among them and like them, seeing the beauty in every human being.

She became a household name for her good world, she is known as the "nun who helped the poor". In 1946 as she travelled to Darjeeling, India for a retreat, she realized what her true calling was "to follow Christ into the slums to serve him among the poorest of the poor." Teresa's first year in the slums was particularly hard, she had to beg for food and supplies for herself and the poor she was serving but she was determined to get herself through it. She taught children to read and write by writing in the dirt with sticks, she visited families, inquiring about their needs and helping provide for them when she could. Her work began to inspire other people who rallied to help. In 1950, she started a mission dedicated to caring for the poorest of the poor, people who feel unwanted, unloved and uncared. As a result, she was honoured with many awards throughout her life of which the Nobel Peace Prize in 1971. She continued her work with the poor for the rest of her life until she died in 1997.By giving others the dignity they needed, she lives a fulfilled and purposeful life inspiring millions of people till today.

Like Mother Theresa, your focus must be people: serving, helping, loving, building and making people better. More women ought to think of themselves as philanthropists. Women generally are more generous than men. Really? Yes!!!! I suspect you are already in the habit to give your time, money and/or skills to a good cause. Am I guessing right? Women tend to be more empathetic and caring than men, factors that affect charitable giving. Similarly, women have been shown to be more altruistic than men, and their giving is usually motivated by their desire to make a difference in people's lives.

Consider volunteering, people who commit to volunteer

work are not only contributing to your community and society, improve your skills but also report a heightened sense of well-being, improved sleep and a stronger immune system. What local causes can you support? Have you taken the time to find out about the charities which are making a difference in your local area? Schools, churches, community centres and community groups usually need volunteers to advance their work. Where does your heart feel the most? Personally, my compassion tends to be more inclined to children. Since I became a Christian it has become apparent that of one my life purpose was to make a difference in children and young people's life. How did I find out? Simply, one day God spoke. A lady Pastor from Canada was on the phone with me and she said, guided by the Spirit of God that I was going to serve amongst children and young people. Imagine my reaction at the time! That came out of the blue. I did not expect it. Far from it! Children? I thought: what have I got to offer to children, let alone young people? I was brought up as a sole child so not got the habit to look after siblings except for changing my nephews' nappies and doing some babysitting here and there!! It's interesting how your brain automatically tuned into and start looking for adequacies and asking: am I qualify to do that? When presenting with an opportunity!! I had no professional experiences or qualifications to work with children, then and no desires or passion to do so. So, I wondered, children? Why not women? After all, I am a woman so why wouldn't I get involved in a women's work instead? Little did I know that when God declares and reveals a thing, it is settled.

Guess what happened? One day, out of the blue, as I was walking down my street from work, I will never forget that day, as if it was yesterday! I lived in Thurrock then, Essex, I came across a group of secondary school children, walking down the street, chatting out loud, have a laugh, like most of them do. And as I looked towards them, my heart started to beat fast for some reasons. I started to feel compassionate for them, it was as if someone was opening my heart wide and pouring some strong empathy for them. Since that I have understood that God was making me feel His compassion for children as a sign that He wanted me to get involved and make a difference in their lives. What is compassion? Compassion literally means "to suffer together." It is a feeling that arises when you are confronted with another's suffering and feel motivated to do something about it! Little did I know that God had it all planned for me, He started to orchestrate circumstances and opportunities for me to get involved.

One day, I remember in 2005, again out of the blue, God spoke to me clearly from the Bible through a Scripture asking me to quit my job. Back then, I was working on my very first permanent job as an Export Commercial with a blue-chip company. I had only been in the job for 18 months, but during that period, a series of life-changing events occurred: I became a Christian, got baptized, started going to Church, spilt from an old boyfriend, and got married. All these in the space of 18 months! Imagine, I had just been in the country for 4 months, freshly arrived from France! My life took a completed turning point as soon as I stepped into the UK! Somehow that tells that God has a pre-defined plan for each of us, He knows the place you meant to be to manifest your purpose, and mine was not France (where I was born) but the UK! I was unaware of His plans for my life until it unfolded bits by bits as I learnt how to hear Him speaks to me. Because I had the habit of reading the bible and praying every day, God started speaking to me through some of the stories, like the one about Abraham, whom God told to leave his country to the land he will be shown and the story of Moses, whom God ordered to go to Egypt to rescue his people from Pharaoh; like Moses I felt inadequate when God said He will use me to work with children.

Guess what! It doesn't matter how I felt because whatever God has called me to be and to do, He knows how to

65

equip me to do it! So, to cut a long story short, I started to get involved working with children, not by my own choice, but people started to pull me into it and recognized I had something to offer and all I have been doing ever since is to step in to seize opportunities God would place right before my eyes. I started volunteering in my local Church, teaching young people, organizing activities for children, working in clubs, and schools. One day God led me to write my life mission statement: "To help young people discover and achieve their life given purpose." I have by the grace of God impacted the lives of hundreds of children and young people locally through various projects, initiatives and work as a Teacher and my dream is to set up a Leadership Academy to help young Leaders become the Eagles in our society.

I've never felt so fulfilled in my life until I discovered my reason for being "my purpose" and getting involved to make a difference with the love and compassion of God has not only benefited others but me as the same time. I have discovered so much about myself, inner gifts, talents, abilities, desires; tapped into opportunities I never thought I would come across; and it is just the beginning of greater things to come.

So, if you feel unfulfilled where you are right now, I urge you to discover God's purpose for your life and get involved to genuinely help other people. As you do, you will be doing yourself a favour, allowing you to discover your true essence and live your life to your full potential with God's help.

Give people what they want

"You can get everything you want in life if you help others get enough of what they want." -Zig Ziglar

If you want to achieve your goals, help others achieve theirs. That's the golden rule of reciprocity. Experience shows that you need to help others reach their dreams if you want to reach yours. Research shows that even if the rewards aren't immediately apparent, contributing to the success of others pays off in the long run. Consider this as a mother, the time you spend looking after your children, educating and caring for them now will pay off later. You reap what you sow! The chances are, if you dedicate quality time with your children to help them to be the best they can be, as they grow older, they will be thankful to you and will be looking for ways to reward you for your hard work and commitment. Your children are your reward for tomorrow. Invest in them.

Think about the people around you, who can you help? Giving your time, money or energy to help others not only make the world a better place but it also makes you better. Studies indicate that the very act of helping other people boosts your happiness, health, and sense of well-being and fulfilment.

If you are looking for more meaning in your day-to-day existence, volunteering and helping others to achieve what they want will enhance your overall sense of purpose and identity. In the course of working at your profession or business, look for ways to help other people you get in contact with on a daily basis. Is there a colleague at work that you can help to perform better, sharing simple tips and advice? It won't cost you anything, just a willingness to help.

Be willing to share knowledge and resources, find out what matters to other people, and make people aware of opportunities around them. These simple things you do to them can go a long way!

Consider this "Successful women help each other."
Do you want to see other women succeed? Are you creating synergies with other women to get ahead?

I love connecting with people; it's like a second nature. I do simple things in the course of running my business, like meeting other people over a cuppa to find out where they are at and see how I can support them. I love networking and get into projects with people and looking back, I realize that through being available to help others, I have come across some many new opportunities I never thought I would.

If you are a woman in business, look for ways to help your partners and customers to have a great experience working with you. Bring humanity in your delivery, find ways to serve your customers' and partners' needs better Be willing to go the extra mile for them and chances are they will go the extra mile for you!

My good friend Arinola who has written the foreword you read at the beginning is the Director and Founder of an Award Winning Financial Education & Financial literacy social enterprise called BMoneywize. She came up with the idea some years ago as a result of her daughter cooking the Nigerian dish "Jollof rice" whenever her friends visited. Arinola then desperate to stop her daughter's enthusiasm for spending every available penny to feed her friends, took the matter into her hands, and thought, 'how can I go about talking to young people about managing money in a fun way so they understand how it is to live on a budget and spend wisely! "So, she gathered her daughter and friends around yet another bowl of Jollof rice and developed BMoneyWize, an interactive and fun board game! Today she has not only solved her own problem, but the problem of hundreds of families in her local area.

Like Arinola, you have the potential within you to find solutions to your problems and as you do, you will be helping other people along the way. Learn to think outside the box, meaning think differently, from a new perspective. Whenever you are facing a challenge; don't focus on the problem, but on the solution. Think how you could use your creativity to come up with an innovative way of solving that problem. Create the WOW factor! Don't just do what most people will do, but tap into your full potential and leave your unique footprint! Which of you as a person is facing challenges? Do you tend to see a glass half-full or half empty? How can you cultivate the ability to look positively?

Are things different from the way you typically look at things in your personal life, professional or business life? A friend of mine has an acute problem-solving sense, working with her on projects is always a piece of cake. Each time we have a challenge, she will suggest a way round it. We worked perfectly together as I am more of a common sense" inspirational thinker, and she has the analytic, problem thinking solves mind. So, we feed on each other's quite well.

Well, one way to boost your performance as far as your personal development, profession and business are concerned is to boost your thinking up to and beyond its limit every now and again. For example, simple ways will be to study another industry, I did that to understand my business industry a bit more and as a result, today, I have decided to acquire new skill sets to complement what I do and help more people find solutions to their problems. That might give you ideas for innovative partnerships, you will also learn how other entrepreneurs in a different industry find solutions to their problem; you could pick up new strategies. Take classes or a course to learn a new topic.

Nationally, about 29 percent of self-employed people are women. In the USA, women represent more than 1/3 of all people involved in entrepreneurial activity. I always wanted to be in business; I dreamt it since I was young. The reason is I always wanted to be in control of what I do with my time; and be in business gives me that flexibility and the freedom to decide how and when and whom I work with. If you are a female entrepreneur or aspire to be, my advice to you is that you start looking within yourself; assess your skills; identify what your passion is and let it lead you to your profession. Your passion for a thing will be solving some else's problem. Find out what you like doing and let people pay you for it!

Margaret Thatcher was an inspiration. She showed that women cannot only survive in a man's world, but also lead it. In 1948, she applied for a job at a company called ICI, the personnel department rejected her application and reported "This woman is headstrong, obstinate and dangerously self-opinionated." Despite the multiple setbacks; later, she went on to become Britain's first female prime minister.

It does not matter what people think of you or reject you. Be obstinate, keep your head up and chase your dreams!

CONCLUSION

Take action today! Become an uncommon woman with an uncommon life. Remove the blocks that prevent you from thriving. Remove the distractions so you can focus on what you really want. Connect to your heart and let your heart guide you to be happy and share your talents and love with the world. This shift will lead to a fulfilled and happy life. Live and achieve at your highest potential!

Finally, keep this in mind: You have infinite potential to achieve anything you want. You just need to stop underestimating yourself and discover your true inner strength. You will find within you an unlimited capacity to achieve.

Being a woman is a blessing from God. Being a woman is a treasure. We women are strong and we are not so easily broken by circumstances of life. We cry in our hearts. Yet we retain beautiful smiles on our faces. We are overcomers. There is no situation that we cannot handle. People may hate us, but we remain strong and beautiful. We are like roses that stay red forever, that will never dry!

The growth is within you, the Extraordinary Woman!

With love,

Miss Purple

AUTHOR BIOGRAPHY

One meeting with Muriel Kakoni is enough to make you feel revived and energized. The beautiful, exuberant woman, also known as Miss Purple has a refreshing presence which brings joy to all she meets. It's no wonder that she is a coach.

Muriel is of French-Caribbean heritage (from the islands Guadeloupe and Martinique). She was born and raised in Paris, France and she has lived in London for over 10 years.

Muriel has a degree in International Business which she gained from the London Metropolitan University. She held roles in various companies, before deciding to launch her own business in 2013. Entrepreneurship is in her blood. Her Grandfather owned a carpentry business, and her sister runs her own successful business back in the Caribbean.

Muriel literally stumbled across the Forever Living brand whilst starting her own weight loss journey. She was so impressed with their products that she decided to become a rep for the network marketing company, and whilst there are many misconceptions around network marketing, Muriel is proud to be associated with the company because she believes in their products.

As well as promoting the Forever Living products, Muriel helps ambitious, entrepreneurial and purpose-driven women live an extraordinary life, inspire, educate and empower them to make better lifestyle choices, look and feel great from the inside-out. She is committed to helping like-minded women take care of themselves and enjoy total freedom and she is very passionate about it. Muriel is a walking, talking advert for what she does. There is a saying - do what you love, and love what you do. Muriel is living her dream, and it is her aim to help thousands of women worldwide to do the same. To live a fulfilled, healthy and happy life, based on their own terms. The future is bright. The future is purple!

You can contact Muriel on info@murielkakoni.com and visit her website: murielkakoni.co.uk

Sign up for her online course **"FREEDOM PILLARS"** - to help you free yourself from the mind blocks that are holding you and your life back from getting the success you know you're meant for.

Visit:
murielkakoni.co.uk
misspurplegroup.com

Engage with her and other readers, post your reviews @ www.facebook.com/misspurplewrites

https://www.facebook.com/misspurplewrites/